I0429178

ABANDONING ABORTION

MY JOURNEY FROM PRO-CHOICE TO PRO-LIFE
& WHY YOU SHOULD MAKE THE SWITCH

Abandoning Abortion

COVER IMAGE

Nicolas Poussin - The Judgment of Solomon - https://
upload.wikimedia.org/wikipedia/commons/0/00/Nicolas_Poussin_-
_The_Judgment_of_Solomon_-_WGA18330.jpg

DEDICATED TO MY WIFE, MARANATHA TOWNSEND, IN ACKNOWLEDGMENT OF THE SACRIFICES SHE MADE FOR THIS BOOK TO BE WRITTEN.

LETTER FROM THE AUTHOR

Dear Reader,

Abortion is a terribly sensitive subject- for good reason. As we will discover in this book, lives are on the line. Our response to this issue has consequences for millions upon millions of people and generations upon generations. I spent the majority of my life in favor of allowing women to decide if abortion was "right for them." I was, what many call, pro-choice. That is no longer the case. What I have seen and learned has informed my new position. I am convinced that there are few issues of greater importance to our current time. In an age that espouses freedoms, rights, and justices, we are dangerously misguided in our treatment of the most vulnerable in our society. Please, enter this discussion with an open mind. Consider the evidences and respond accordingly. As Edmund Burke famously noted, "The only thing necessary for the triumph of evil is for good men[and women] to do nothing."

In Love,
Chris Townsend

INTRODUCTION

Abortion may be one of the most divisive issues of our time. This is not without reason. If abortion is really killing human lives, then we are killing millions of babies each year and calling it good. If abortion does not kill human lives, then women are being restricted from a potentially helpful medical procedure. It stands to reason then, that we should do everything in our power to determine whether or not abortion really does kill babies - and just to be safe, we should always err on the side of caution when potentially dealing with innocent lives. We will consider questions of life, value, and many of the political arguments made against pro-life positions. The discoveries are startling. Attempts to validate abortion as an ethical activity must deny science, reason, and common sense. I spent the majority of my life as pro-choice. However, the information found in this book changed my mind. What I discovered has shaken me to my core and caused me to pick up the mantle of protecting the lives of our unborn children. As Oxford philosopher, Ravi Zacharias, has eloquently stated, "The ultimate test of any civilization is how we treat the most vulnerable... what we do to our children. Our world has lost its direction."[1]

DISCLAIMER

Abortion is a terribly sensitive subject. The majority of this book will deal with the realities of abortion. As such, it is bound to push on people's sensitivities. Furthermore, according to Planned Parenthood statistics, over thirty percent of women have an abortion by the time they are forty-five.[2] It is reasonable then, to assume assume that many of the women reading this will have had an abortion and many of the men reading this will have played a part in an abortion as well. With this in mind, it is important that you understand what I am saying, what I am not saying, why I am saying it, and what I want you to know from the start.

---

[1] Ravi Zacharias, "Twitter," Twitter, August 22, 2015, accessed December 10, 2015, https://twitter.com/ravizacharias/status/635099200347201537.

[2] "Abortion," Planned Parenthood, accessed December 10, 2015, https://www.plannedparenthood.org/learn/abortion.

MY REQUEST

Few people enter this conversation unencumbered by strong presupposed positions. Even if you have not studied the arguments of each side before, chances are that you hold a fairly strong view, if for no other reason than you are part of a culture that holds strong views about this topic. As a point of fact, when we hold strong positions on a given topic we are often resistant to information that could alter our position. I beg of you, we are dealing with human lives (either that of the mother or that of the mother and the child). This should not be taken lightly and we should not allow our predispositions to dictate the outcome of our conclusions.

A BRIEF WORD ON MORALITY

This book seeks to answer one simple question: Is abortion morally wrong? Of course to answer this question we must first dispel with the all-too-common idea of subjective morality, which suggests that "what is right for you is right for you and what is right for me is right for me." If these statements are true, then we cannot answer the questions about right and wrong because no such objective statement can be made about anything - all morality, according to this perspective is subjective. If subjective morality is correct, then you can't tell someone that having an abortion is wrong and they can't tell you that stopping an abortion is wrong. Of course, common sense tells us that this is not the case. Ultimately, actions are either right or they are wrong. Trying to pass legislation to restrict abortion access is either right or wrong. Having an abortion is either right or wrong. If you are not convinced by this short explanation on morality, please consider reading the chapter of *Prove It: The Art & Science of Understanding Why You Believe What You Believe* that deals with morality. It goes into greater detail.

WHAT I AM SAYING

In the unlikely event that the title of this book did not give away the conclusion, here it is: Abortion is wrong. To arrive at this conclusion, we will look at three basic claims:

1. We have a moral responsibility to protect innocent human life.
2. Abortion ends innocent human life.
3. Therefore, **we have a moral responsibility to protect innocent human lives from abortion.**

WHAT I AM NOT SAYING

I am not condemning people who have been pro-choice, pro-abortion, or even those who have, themselves had an abortion or provided abortion services.

WHY AM I SAYING THIS?

As I just mentioned, I am not saying this to be cruel to anyone. I am not saying it to offend, condemn, or even rebuke. I am saying it with one goal in mind - the future - specifically the future lives of millions of preborn babies. What is done is done. I myself have been complicit in much harm in the past. Though I am not proud of many of my past actions, I do not dwell on them, feel condemned for them, and **I certainly would not dwell on, or condemn, you for your past.** I believe the best way to fix the future is through education. **This book**, while dealing with difficult, sensitive and emotion-evoking truths **is not an indictment of your past. Rather it is a message of hope for the future.**

WHAT I WANT YOU TO KNOW

It may be difficult to distinguish between my condemnation of abortion and my lack of condemnation of those who have had an abortion in the past. To understand how this is possible, you must understand that I am approaching this all from a decidedly Christian perspective. While that has some bearing on my opinion about abortion, it has a greater impact on my opinion about the mothers, fathers, and even doctors who have chosen to participate in abortion. In the event that you have not been told, foundational to Christianity is the doctrine of salvation (formally known as soteriology). While an in-depth discussion of salvation doctrine is beyond the scope of this book, a simple explanation will suffice for now and here it is: Jesus Christ offers forgiveness to everyone.

There is no sin too great for the forgiveness of God. If you are capable of believing in such a forgiving God,[3] then this is certainly the best offer you can ever hope to receive. That is why it is called the Gospel, which literally means "good news." Even if you have participated in killing your own child, knowingly or unknowingly, even if you are a doctor who has performed thousands of

---

[3] Again, if this seems untenable, read Prove It: The Art & Science of Understanding & Articulating Why You Believe What You Believe. Hopefully the many chapters in that book will empower you to recognize that belief in such a God is at least rationally plausible if not rationally necessary.

abortions, God offers you forgiveness. But the offer does not just stop at forgiveness. Most theologians would agree, that God offers you a hope to know your child in heaven. You must simply accept that forgiveness.

For some, this is immensely difficult. For me, it was exceedingly simple. Once I believed in God, I knew full well how awful I had been, how much harm I had done to people, and how deserving I was of judgment. Perhaps I am a bit of a self-protecting pragmatist, but the moment I heard someone mention forgiveness, I hopped on the forgiveness train without a second thought. I had never heard an offer so good. A chance to be forgiven, to know God now and into eternity, is the greatest offer anyone could ask for. God wants you to know that NO SIN IS TOO GREAT. Isaiah 1:18 tells us, "Come now, let us reason together, says the LORD: though your sins are like scarlet, they shall be as white as snow; though they are red like crimson, they shall become like wool." God offers you forgiveness. I want you to know this ,because it has changed my life. I want you to know this, because I want you to know that I am truly not condemning you, but I do want to prevent future pain and so I will, with my life, fight to educate you about the realities of abortion.

WHY IS THIS NOTEWORTHY?

Because this is a very difficult topic and it is vital that you don't hear condemnation from what I say. Denial is a powerful enemy of truth and I have seen people choose to pretend that something is not wrong(denial) so as to protect themselves from feeling condemnation. I, myself, am on that list. But, know this, there is no condemnation to those who are in Christ Jesus (Romans 8:1). You need not be afraid of your past actions and you need not hide from the terrible things you may have done, whatever they may be. **Let it go(God has), seek truth, and receive forgiveness.**

TESTIMONY
Introduction

Lest ye think I am just an "indoctrinated conservative Christian" from birth, tis fitting that I present my own testimony. I was a pro-choice agnostic until I was twenty-five. Clearly, these are no longer the case. The Bible tells Christians that we should always be prepared to give a reason for the hope that we have (1Pt 3:16). As such, I want to share with you what changed *my* mind about abortion. I don't expect this section to change your mind, but I want you to understand what happened and why I fight so ardently for the lives of preborn babies.

Why Was I Pro-Choice?

Simply put, my perspective was a product of my environment. Pro-choice is what I had been taught. Through television, music, and personal relationships, pro-choice was presented as the only rational, ethical, and therefore appropriate perspective. I never bothered to look into it. It just was what it was - the right choice was pro-choice. Anyone else was a close-minded misogynist. The perspective seemed simple enough. I wanted women to be able to choose what to do with their bodies. I wanted to empower women and if they wanted to abort some unformed cells, who was I to say what they could or couldn't do?

There was something else at play though. Not only did I come out looking like a hero for being "pro-women," there were other perks to the perspective. You see, we have a culture that likes sex, lots of sex, and I was no different. I was part of the hookup culture- the kind of culture that goes out to the bars and clubs with the intent of finding a sex partner. The interesting thing about this hookup culture is that it likes to sweep consequences under the rug. By giving women the "choice," I was effectively removing my personal responsibility. I would not have thought of it that way at the time, and I would not have admitted to it had someone confronted me about it, but the fact is, it was far easier to be a man in the hookup culture and have an exit strategy should pregnancy occur. Not only this, but I wouldn't really have to be the one responsible for "deciding." After all, that's the whole point of the movement; it's a woman's choice. It was awfully convenient for me to simply regurgitate what I had heard, "men have no say over what women do with their bodies." Such a perspective places the responsibility of birth control and sexuality on the woman. It allows for male complacency. So long as it was consensual I could participate in any sexual activity without having to be totally concerned about the consequences of potential pregnancy. This is a shameful and abhorrent perspective, and one that I am not proud of, but there it is. Women were, among other things, an opportunity for pleasure, and a pro-choice position curried favor with women while simultaneously distancing myself from responsibility. Or so I thought...

What Changed My Mind?

Interestingly enough, it was actually being put into a possible abortion situation that made me change my mind. There are so many evils and difficulties in this world that **we often don't consider positions fully until they face us personally- it was a personal brush with abortion that caused me to shift from pro-choice to pro-life.**

I was twenty-five at the time. I had just moved to a new city and was quite lonely. A married friend of mine had become disconnected from her husband and we began sleeping together. I was not yet a Christian, nor did I believe in God, but I knew it was wrong to sleep with a married woman. I would even try to stop the relationship at various times. Then the lonely feeling would come back and one thing would lead to another and we'd find ourselves in inappropriate situations time after time. This carried on for a month or two (I don't remember the exact timeline).

Then something interesting happened. I had an encounter that convinced me to go back to church and give God a chance again. The first service I went to was a college group service and the preacher spoke about the emotional/spiritual consequences of extramarital and premarital sex. He talked about the connections that are made in sexual encounters and the pain and damage that occurs when those connections are torn apart. As surprising as it may sound to some, I had never heard anything like this in my entire life. I was always just warned about STDs and pregnancy and I knew that my parents didn't want me to have sex outside of marriage, but I never really understood the "Why" behind the command.

The message hit home. I thought back over my long list of encounters and considered the pain and harm that I had experienced and caused to others through years of sexual activity. I thought about the manipulative things girls had done to me and the manipulative things I had done to them. The entire hookup lifestyle is fraught with distrust, insecurity, and pain. While I wasn't ready to swear off the sex entirely, I thought I'd start taking a step back and pause on actual sexual intercourse for a while.

Little did I know, it was too late. One day, while talking to my best friend on the phone, I got a text message: "I'm pregnant." It was from the married friend of mine that I had been sleeping with.

I wasn't her only extramarital partner, so we didn't know who the child's father was, but we knew that she was pregnant. I was heartbroken, afraid, and ashamed. I had played with fire one too many times, and this time something serious had happened. Forget about all of the harmful relationships, risking STDs and all sorts of other dangers, this was a child we were talking about and the mother was married to another man. Of course, being pro-choice my initial thought would be abortion. As it turns out the other men involved wanted an abortion as well. However, in spite of my personal desire to be free of the responsibilities associated with the child, something inside me changed. For some reason, almost as if a voice spoke to me, I knew in my heart and mind that if there was even a chance the child was mine I could not let an abortion occur.

This shift in perspective confounds reason. I was pro-choice. I felt horrible about what I had done. A child would almost certainly seal the fate of their marriage. I would unquestionably incur significant financial responsibility and I wasn't going to let the child go without her father. I didn't want to be involved with the mother in that way. I didn't want to tell my future wife and children that I had another family. I didn't have the money to help support the child. An abortion was the only reasonable option and yet something inside me told me that it wasn't reasonable at all. I had never really considered what a child looked like in the womb. I had never considered that it might really be life; but, for some reason, I knew that the abortion would be wrong.

Not knowing how to handle this apparent revelation, I went to the pastor who had begun helping me in this new season and transition. I told him that I felt God was telling me not to go forward with an abortion. After I shared my thoughts, he agreed with me. I told him that I didn't know what to do - that all of the other men were pushing her for an abortion. He told me about pregnancy centers that would get her the full information about abortions, show her an ultrasound, etc. She agreed to go and left feeling convicted that an abortion was not a real option. **She made the brave choice to keep the baby despite the pressure from the other men.**

Still, I don't know that I would have considered myself pro-life at this point. I was not personally educated on the realities of abortion. I hadn't heard God say that abortion was wrong in general. I had only heard about my own personal situation and I was probably still under the impression that it was ethical for adults to make decisions about the lives of their babies.

Sometime later, I came across pictures of babies in the womb and eventually pictures of post-aborted babies. Once I realized what abortion really was, I *knew* it was wrong, not just in my case, but in all cases -with debatably one exception, which we will address later. For the first time in my life, it struck me, "This is really a human being that we are talking about." From that point on, I decided to study the issues. Needless to say, I was shocked by what I found out.

THE SHORT ANSWER

Here is what my research led me to discover:

1. We have a moral responsibility to protect innocent human life.

2. Abortion ends innocent human life: science recognizes each human child, from embryonic stages, as a genetically distinct human life. It is not the mother's body. Babies are their own being from the point of fertilization.

3. Therefore, **we have a moral responsibility to protect innocent human lives from abortion.** - just as we would protect any other human being.

Exploring those, and other arguments for and against abortion will follow for the remainder of the book. I hope that my experience and research will help shed light on the issue for you and help you to approach conversations with other in a healthy and effective manner. Whether you are currently pro-life, pro-abortion, or something else, the topics found in the rest of this book can help you better understand the harsh realities of abortion.

CLEARING THE AIR
Dealing With The Uncomfortable Reality

There is an underlying element that influences people, often subconsciously. I know it was working within me for many years. I believe it even influences even the most ardent pro-life advocates. It is a numbing agent that separates us from the realities of abortion: **If abortion is really killing human babies, then we are killing thousands (roughly 4-5k in our country alone) babies each and every day.** In fact, several have been killed in the time its taken you to read this paragraph. That is a pretty intense thing to consider and I think a lot of us simply assume that we, as a society, wouldn't do something so evil and so we automatically disregard the possibility that abortion is homicide, because, if abortion is, in fact, homicide, then we are doing something irrevocably atrocious on a massive scale. Think of it this way, if we killed millions of born babies each year, what kind of response do you imagine would follow? There is unquestionably some kind of mental barrier to recognizing this worldwide infanticide for what it truly is. Nevertheless, whatever the conclusion, we must cast aside preconceptions and attempt to dismantle unfounded mental barriers.

CLEARING OUT LANGUAGE

I have had many conversations with pro-choice and pro-abortion advocates. I have noticed a trend in language confusion. I say one thing and they hear something else. We must distinguish certain linguistic tricks that our minds can play before we begin this conversation. Understand, as I often note in my books, that language is a relative expression of our absolute reality. In other words, truth is objective and outside of our control, but we can all use words differently. I can use a word to mean something different than you use it. Likewise, even if we are using a word to mean generally the same thing, that word has different qualifiers and triggers than it may for me.

Therefore, for example, if I say abortion is murder, you might say, "no it's not, because it's not against the law." Some confusion exists in this statement. I am not saying that abortion is legally recognized as premeditated homicide. I am saying that it is ethically murder regardless of legal recognition.

A parallel exists in the slave trades of old. Legally, slaves were viewed as subhuman and therefore any number of crimes could be committed against them with legal impunity. Murder, in some cases, was not considered murder, because killing a slave was not breaking the law. Nevertheless, most (I hope) would agree today that those killings were, in fact, murder, regardless of what the law said. It is important to recognize that within this book, I am not, unless otherwise specified, referring to current legal definitions. Remember, the law is meant to be built on ethics; ethics are not based on the law. **It is never appropriate to assume that the law is the standard for morality** -if the law is the standard for morality, then slavery was moral, the holocaust was moral, marital abuse was moral, etc.

ADDRESSING THE ISSUE OF LIFE
What Are We Really Trying To Determine?

Ultimately, when it comes to abortion there is one question at stake: "are preborn babies human lives?" **If preborn babies are human lives, then ethically we cannot, for any reason, kill them.** I am going to assume that you agree with that statement as most rational adults would.[4] No argument for abortion could stand up if, in fact, we are dealing with a human life. The only way a pro-choice argument can stand up to reason, is if preborn babies are considered less than human beings.

What Is A Human?

A human is a man, woman, or child of the species homo sapiens.[5] Notice that there is no developmental distinction. A human does not magically become human when it is born, capable of surviving outside of a womb,

---

[4] Of course there are always extreme cases. For example, "If we abort this baby, somehow it will stop a nuclear bomb from going off." While these extreme answers are always possible, in most normal cases, killing an innocent human person is not an ethically acceptable option.

[5] Oxford Dictionaries, s.v. "Human Being," accessed December 10, 2015, http://www.oxforddictionaries.com/us/definition/american_english/human-being.

or any other arbitrary developmental stage. A human is a human. We can add qualifiers like a human woman, a human man, a human child, a human infant, a human embryo, etc. However, these do not change the humanity of the subject.

Are Preborn Babies Human In Nature?

There is no scientific question that even prior to conception, both the sperm and the egg are human in nature. They are not camel, rabbit, plant, etc. They are human.

Are Preborn Baby's Life?

Again, there is no scientific question about whether or not we are discussing life. Unquestionably, even embryos are alive. If we found a single celled organism on Mars, the whole world would erupt in chatter over the discovery of life. There is no question that the multi celled embryo is life - and human life at that! As Professor Micheline Mathews-Roth of Harvard University medical School says "It is scientifically correct to say that an individual human life begins at conception."[6] Even

---

[6] Randy C. Alcorn, Why Pro-Life? Caring for the Unborn and Their Mothers, Rev ed. (Albany: Hendrickson Pub, 2012), 27.

Oregon's largest abortion clinic testified under oath, "Of course human life begins at conception."[7]

Are Preborn Babies Part Of The Mother's Body?

No, from the moment of conception, the preborn baby, even in embryonic form is genetically distinct from his or her mother. Yes, they live within the body of the mother, but no they are not part of her body. Dr. Jerome LeJune former genetics professor at the University of Descartes in Paris has stated, "After fertilization has taken place a new human being has come into being... this is no longer a matter of taste or opinion. Each individual has a very neat beginning at conception."[8]

At this point, things should be pretty clear. The conversation should probably end. Preborn human babies are genetically distinct human beings from the moment of fertilization. Causing the death of one of them is, by definition, homicide.

However, as we will see, the conversation does not often end here. Those in favor of abortion have

[7] Randy C. Alcorn, Why Pro-Life? Caring for the Unborn and Their Mothers, Rev ed. (Albany: Hendrickson Pub, 2012), 27.

[8] Randy C. Alcorn, Why Pro-Life? Caring for the Unborn and Their Mothers, Rev ed. (Albany: Hendrickson Pub, 2012), 27.

attempted, with every effort, to get around the idea that abortion is wrong. Regardless of the fact that this is a human being's life that is being ended, many additional requirements have been added by abortionists to validate abortion. We will look at them all and see that though the questions shouldn't even have to be asked, not one of the stretched reasons for abortion validates abortion as acceptable. Whatever arbitrary and manipulative language we couch the conversation in, at the end of the day, abortion still causes the death of a human life.

Initial Conclusion: Abortion Is Homicide.

Homicide is when one human being causes the death of another.[9] Many call abortion murder, and I have as well. While this may be true in some sense, it is not technically murder as, legally speaking, "murder occurs when one human being unlawfully kills another human being." Technically, abortion is legal, so it's not, definitionally speaking, murder. At the same time, as we have seen, abortion is, by definition, homicide, as it is a

---

[9] "Homicide," Cornell Law Legal Information Institute, accessed December 10, 2015, https://www.law.cornell.edu/wex/homicide.

human being causing the death of another human being. Remember, laws don't dictate ethics; ethics dictate laws.

PRO-CHOICE ARGUMENTS BEYOND LIFE
Attempting To Draw Distinctions In "Personhood"

Nevertheless, those who are determined to make abortion look ethical, attempt to distinguish between preborn children and born children. To help create linguistic differences between the preborn and born child, many pro-choice advocates evoke the language of personhood.

However, a study of personhood quickly shows that any attempt to distinguish between a human being and a human person is entirely subjective, arbitrary, and unscientific. Such attempts are an affront to honest pursuits of truth. Below we will outline some of the many flawed attempts at creating distance between the human being and human person. Proabortionists argument for personhood generally take on one of four basic forms as represented by the acronym SLED (Size, Level of Development, Environment, Degree of Dependency). Before we get into that, we must look at the concept of personhood.

What Is A Person Anyway?

Merriam-Webster simply define a person as "a human being."[10] Oxford Dictionary adds a qualifier, "A human being regarded as an individual."[11] They go on to define an individual "A single human being as distinct from a group, class, or family."[12] Again, not that these definitions actually have creative power, but even from a definitional perspective, "human being" is the primary qualifier. Some form of distinction from a group, class, or family has been added to this particular definition.

However, it matters not, because we as people, don't have the ability to define ourselves - not really. We must recognize our limitations as humans. Truth is *not* subjective, even if our interpretation of a single and universal truth *is* subjective. Ultimately there is a singular reality and though we have the power to change our

---

[10] Merriam-Webster Dictionary, s.v. "Person," accessed December 10, 2015, http://www.merriam-webster.com/dictionary/person

[11] Oxford Dictionaries, s.v. "Person," accessed December 10, 2015, http://www.oxforddictionaries.com/us/definition/american_english/person.

[12] Oxford Dictionaries, s.v. "individual," accessed December 10, 2015, http://www.oxforddictionaries.com/us/definition/american_english/individual.

language, our language does not have the power to change our reality - only our perception of that reality. In other words, language is a relative expression of absolute truth.

For example, we have the power to define a person as a born human being. Likewise, we could define a person as a goat or a chair. This one may sound familiar: We can define a person as a white male. Can we make such definitions? Certainly. Do such definitions make preborn babies less human? Do they make goats and chairs people or blacks, hispanics, asians, and women not persons? Of course not. The point is simple. We lack the capacity to change reality with our definitions. All that we can do is use language to categorize and explain the reality that already exists. And that reality makes no rational value distinction between preborn and born human beings. To confirm, let's look over SLED.

SLED
Size:
Does Size Determine Personhood?

Even the most ardent pro-abortion advocate will have to admit that size has nothing to do with whether something is a human life. Newly born children are no less human beings than their adult selves. Nor are short or skinny people less human than their taller or heavier counterparts. Does how big you are determine your humanity, your personhood, or your worth? Of course not.

Level Of Development:
Does Level Of Development Determine Personhood?

Again, this is an arbitrary division. The concept of full development is an illusion. Life is in a constant state of flux. At what point would one be considered "fully developed?" Even attempting to claim fully developed as an adult is a slippery slope as the elderly are developed differently than someone in their twenties, thirties, or even forties, fifties, and sixties. Life's development is never stagnant. It is always reshaping, adding, and sometimes subtracting. There is no single static state that can be successfully described as "fully developed."

Even if we could point to some stage of life and say, "That is fully developed," that stage would not occur until some form of adulthood. Therefore, the argument for development would allow for killing infants, children, and even teenagers based on the concept that they are not yet "fully developed."

Dr. Alfred M. Bongioanni, professor of obstetrics at University of Pennsylvania states it as such, "I have learned from my earliest medical education that human life begins at the time of conception... human life is present throughout the entire sequence from conception to adulthood... any interruption at any point throughout this time constitutes a termination of human life... I am no more prepared to say that these early stages represent an incomplete human being than I would be to say that the child prior to the dramatic effects of puberty is not a human being. This is human life at every stage."[13]

Environment:
Does Being In the Mother's Womb Mean Their Life Is Not Worthy Of Protection?

What does location and environment have to do with personhood? Absolutely nothing. Would you consider someone in one country less of a person than people in another country? Are astronauts less of a person when they go into outers pace? Is someone less of a person when they are in a building or outside of a building? No. So, why would someone moving (only inches) out of their

---

[13] Randy C. Alcorn, Why Pro-Life? Caring for the Unborn and Their Mothers, Rev ed. (Albany: Hendrickson Pub, 2012), 27.

mother's body change their personhood? Environment and location have nothing to do with personhood. Any attempt to use this argument is, again, arbitrary and illogical.

Degree Of Dependency:
Does Dependency On The Mother Determine Personhood?

Preborn babies are dependent upon the mother. However, dependency is another arbitrary and illogical metric for discerning the value of a life. A child is still dependent upon parents once they are born. If independence is the metric we want to use, then it is not just the preborn that we should have the right to kill. Babies, young children, and mentally disabled adults, would all fall into the category of killable, if worth is derived from independence.

Conclusion

Clearly all stages of the acronymous SLED fail to distinguish personhood at some special size, level of development, environmental shift, or degree of dependency. Humans are humans. However, the arguments still continue. We will continue by addressing some of the other common complaints against pro-life positions.

More Stretching
"But They Are Not Capable Of Feeling Pain!"

While some abortion occur before physical pain sensors are developed others abortions occur well after children are capable of feeling pain. Conservative (statistically not politically) estimates suggest that pain is felt by twenty weeks, with response to touch occurring as early as eight weeks.[14]

More importantly, pain is not an appropriate metric for protecting life. For example, if someone has rare congenital insensitivity to pain, we would not say that we should be able to kill them because they can't feel pain. Likewise, we could put someone to sleep using a sleeping pill and then kill them painlessly. Would that be acceptable? Of course not! Likewise, using pain as a metric for killing preborn babies is unacceptable. However, the fact that we literally cut them into pieces within the womb while they are capable of feeling pain is a ghastly and horrendous reality of the abortion industry.

---

[14] "Fetal Pain: The Evidence,", accessed December 10, 2015, http://www.doctorsonfetalpain.com/.

"If You're Pro-Life, Then Why Do You Advocate For The Death Penalty?"

The death penalty argument fails on many accounts. First, it assumes that pro-lifers are in favor of the death penalty, while many are not. Some are ardently opposed to it. Second, as my parents always told me growing up, two wrongs don't make a right. Theoretically, someone making this claim to a pro-life advocate in favor of the death penalty may be pointing out a hypocrisy, but it would not validate either action. If the death penalty is morally reprehensible, it simply points to further error in our legal system. It does not validate abortion. In other words, even if someone is wrong to be in favor of the death penalty, or anything else for that matter, it doesn't make killing preborn babies acceptable. The two have nothing to do with one another. Such claims are the height of irrationality.

Finally, there is a clear distinction between killing innocent preborn children and killing criminals as punishment and protection. Much could be said about this, and I am not suggesting that the death penalty is correct, but there is unquestionably a difference between killing an innocent child and someone who, through legal process has been convicted of some heinous crime, almost unquestionably with some premeditated homicide tied to it. Again, I am not advocating for the death penalty, but claiming a one for one on the two issues is not an accurate parallel.

Therefore, this argument fails on not one, but at least three accounts. It assumes pro-lifers are in favor of the death penalty, even though many are not. The death penalty has nothing to do with whether abortion is right or wrong. Killing babies out of convenience is far different than executing murderers for the sake of legal punishment and protection.

"I'd Be Pro-Life, But There Are So Many Unwanted Children That Nobody Wants To Adopt."

As will always be the case, this doesn't make it acceptable to kill children. Just because they are unwanted does not mean they deserve death. Acting like this is a mercy killing is a huge error. We *do* need help with our adoption system and there are many parents patiently waiting to adopt, but even if there were not, do you really believe that it is rational to kill children because they "aren't wanted?" According to this logic, we should kill all homeless children. Also, as mentioned before, two wrongs don't make a right. There are many pro-lifers who do wonderful work with adoption, adopt or foster children themselves, or participate in adoption advocacy groups. Either way, **extermination is not a valid response to undesired humans.**

"My Body. My Choice."

We have already exposed the logical and scientific fallacies associated with this line of thinking. Simply put, from the moment of fertilization, the baby is a genetically unique human being. In NO WAY is the baby part of the mother's body, even if they are in the mother's body. While there may be implications to the mother's body for carrying the child, the child is not part of the mother's body. **Whatever effect upon the mother's body is being considered, it must be measured plainly against the reality of abortion - the extermination of a life.** Using this statement as an excuse to ignore the implications of abortion is entirely unacceptable. We are talking about a human life. Therefore, the only place that such arguments could be reasonably brought to the table are in relation to the life of the mother. Any other reason is comparing a temporary situation to the premeditated termination of an innocent human life.

"Men Should Shut The Hell Up"[15]

This was an actual statement made by Senator Claire McCaskill. She is not the first, nor will she be the last to suggest that men have no right to participate in the abortion discussion. There are many things that need to be said about such statements.

First and foremost, this is not a "women's" issue. We are dealing with the lives of preborn children, some female, some male. There is more than one life to consider. More eloquently put, **abortion is a human rights issue that extends beyond the desires of the pregnant woman.** Our ethical responsibility involves protecting each and every life, not just those who can speak for themselves. As there are, scientifically speaking, multiple lives at play, it is entirely unethical to disregard the life of a child for the sake of the mother's preference. Cut and dry, men who take a pro-life stance are pro-woman; they are protecting the millions of female girls that are being killed by abortion each year.

---

[15] Zeba Blay, "Claire McCaskill Kindly Encourages Men to 'shut the Hell Up'," Huffington Post, November 2015, 1, accessed Decmber 10, 2015, http://www.huffingtonpost.com/entry/senator-claire-mccaskill-encourages-men-to-just-shut-the-hell-up_us_5642208ce4b0b24aee4be8ac.

Second, the idea that men have no right to speak about women's issues is absurd for many reasons. Granted, men should be educated on women's issues if they are to speak about them, but then again so should women. Attempting to cut out the voice of half the population is a control method, not a rational argument. Such a concept undermines the fabric of society. Every voice has value, be that voice male or female.

Third, contrary to some perspectives, pro-life is not even close to a male led movement. Women are major players in the movement to protect life. Passing pro-life off as misogynistic is a total misrepresentation of the pro-life demographic.

Finally, women taking this stance are indirectly condoning the kind of irresponsible selfishness that I aligned with in my youth. By telling men that they have no right to participate in such conversations, women are giving men a "free out." If this is entirely women's responsibility, then, so long as the sex is consensual, the pregnancy-related consequences are outside of the man's responsibility as well. **Both parents are equally responsible**, even if the woman carries the child.

"I Am Not In Favor Of Abortion, But I Can't Tell Anyone Else What To Do."

This is totally irrational, inconsistent, and neglects to understand that purpose of community governance. Any law or legal restriction is telling others what they can and cannot do. By making the claim that "we can't tell anyone else to do," we are suggesting that we should have no laws. This argument, taken to its logical conclusion, is no less than anarchy. By the reasoning used above, we should not restrict theft, rape, murder, or any other crime against humanity. According to this position, there should be no laws whatsoever.

The only way that this statement can make any sense in the case of abortion is if you can prove that the child is not a distinct human being and is instead a part of the mother's body. We have already confirmed beyond reasonable doubt that such a position is ignorant, flies in the face of scientific fact, and has no foundation in reality. Furthermore, even if it was the mother's body, we still make many laws that restrict actions against oneself. Our culture recognizes that we must protect lives, even from ourselves. We also recognize that private actions have public consequences. This is why we have laws restricting drug abuse, suicide, etc.

"Crime Has Decreased As Unwanted Pregnancies Have Been Terminated."

This statement seems powerful at first, but a closer look recognizes several flaws. First, the economists making such claims are taking a very loose look at a corollary and ascribing causal implications. This is dangerous, misguided, and flagrantly bad statistical analysis. In other words, these "economists" are noting a potential relationship between the timeline of abortion legalization and crime reduction and claiming that there is a direct causal relationship. They should know better than to make such sweeping unsubstantiated claims. Many other factors could have led to the decrease in crime.

Furthermore, by this reasoning, we should just kill all at-risk individuals in order to reduce likelihood of them committing crime. This idea seems more like something you would find in a dystopian science fiction film than something that would be promoted in our culture. Somehow this passes as brilliant economics in our modern culture- scary indeed.

Most importantly, while abortion is not a legal crime, we have recognized that it is a crime against humanity regardless of its legal status. Therefore, while legal statistics show a drop in crime, those statistics fail to recognize the fifty to sixty million abortions/homicides committed in the US during the same time span. Though they may not be illegal, these abortions should be counted as millions of crimes against humanity.

Finally, we have not yet taken into consideration the consequences of those lost lives - the utilitarian value of their presence, or rather lack their of. This must be addressed from at least two angles. First, what if one in that fifty million would have had a cure for cancer, been a revolutionary who shaped nations in goodness, or an inventor who changed the world as we know it. The fact is, we will never know. Second, there are economic consequences associated with birthrates. Economists recognize the consequences of a sub-replacement fertility rate. Look at the chart below. Notice when the sharp drop off occurred in the US (the same time that abortions became legal).

You may not have thought of it this way before, but God's command to

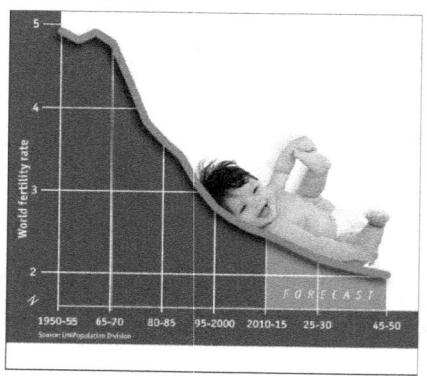

"be fruitful and multiply" was, among other things, an expansive economic requirement. This drastic drop-off in replacement rate is a serious component of our nations unfunded liability debt, which many are predicting could lead to a national economic collapse. I wonder what would happen to the crime rate should that happen?[16]

"People Are Just Going To Have Abortion Anyway. We Have A Responsibility To Make The Process Accessible And Safe."

By this logic, we should help murderers and rapists victimize their prey in safer ways as well. All we have to do is replace abortion with the word homicide to see how foolish this argument really is. "People are just going to commit homicide anyway. We have a responsibility to make the process accessible and safe." People really do commit homicide everyday. Often the process of attacking another person is dangerous to the attacker. By the reasoning used above, we should help protect the attacker simply because they risk harming themselves in the attack.

---

[16] Jonathan Last, "America's Baby Bust," Wall Street Journal (February 2013): 1, www.wsj.com/articles/ SB10001424127887323337520457827005338770718.

INTERESTING FACTS

- Even Norma McCorvey, the woman previously known as Jane Roe (from Roe v. Wade), has reversed her position and is now an outspoken pro-life advocate. **"Back in 1973, I was a very confused twenty-one year old with one child and facing an unplanned pregnancy... At the time I fought to obtain a legal abortion, but truth be told, I have three daughters and never had an abortion... I think it's safe to say that the entire abortion industry is based on a lie.... I am dedicated to spending the rest of my life undoing the law that bears my name."**[17]

- Not only is abortion legal in the United States, but it is publicly funded (even if it is indirect) by our tax dollars. People will say that the money doesn't go toward abortion, but anyone who understands how companies are run will understand that it doesn't matter what that specific money is used for. Money is money. Would you give a drug dealer gas money or money for their house payment or cell phone bill? Of

---

[17] Steven Ertelt, "Woman Behind Roe V. Wade," LifeSiteNews, January 2013, 1, accessed December 10, 2015, http://www.lifenews.com/2013/01/22/woman-behind-roe-v-wade-im-dedicating-my-life-to-overturning-it/.

course not, because even if the money isn't going to purchase drugs, supporting them financially enables them to continue what they are doing. Every dollar you give to the drug dealer, even if it is specified to go to non-drug purchases, frees up more of their other money to go toward drug purchases. Likewise, government money may not go directly to fund abortions, but it does help to keep the doors of abortion providers open. It does fatten the wallets of those who are advocating for and working to provide abortions. Yes, abortion is funded with your money.

- The modern abortion movement was closely tied to population control and negative eugenics, which seeks to speed up natural selection by systematically exterminating weak humans before they can breed. This movement was particularly racist, deeming certain races as inferior and therefore worthy of eugenic extermination. "Some eugenicists separated the "fit" and "unfit" classes along racist and nativist lines. Under this eugenics model, those considered most worthy of rearing children were couples who were middle class or upper class Nordic-Teutonic whites. Racial minorities and ethnic immigrant groups were typically classified as unfit."[18]

CONCLUSION

From the moment of fertilization, babies are genetically distinct human being. There is no rational way to redefine life or the worth of a child. Babies are living human beings from the moment of fertilization. Attempts to alter the worth of unborn babies based on stages, locations, or anything else, fail the test of logic and/or deny the scientific evidence. Abortion is ethically indefensible. We have a responsibility to protect the lives of the unborn. Furthermore, we have a responsibility to educate those who have been fooled into thinking that this is anything other than worldwide infanticide. Please carefully consider the details of this book. If you are pro-life, please consider using some of this information to help educate others on what has become, perhaps, the greatest atrocity of our generations. If you have favored being "pro-choice," I beg you to reconsider in light of the evidence. I know I have given you a lot to think about.

---

[18] "People & Events: Eugenics and Birth Control," PBS, accessed March 11, 2016, http://www.pbs.org/wgbh/amex/pill/peopleevents/e_eugenics.html.

Let that information settle and ask yourself "should abortion really be a choice? Is ending a unique and innocent human life, at any stage of development really an ethically viable decision?" The science and logic are clear. Abortion ends the life of a child. Choose to stand with me and abandon abortion!

BIBLIOGRAPHY

Alcorn, Randy C. Why Pro-Life? Caring for the Unborn and Their Mothers. Rev ed. Albany: Hendrickson Pub, 2012.

Blay, Zeba. "Claire Mccaskill Kindly Encourages Men to 'shut the Hell Up'." Huffington Post, November 2015. Accessed Decmber 10, 2015. http://www.huffingtonpost.com/entry/senator-claire-mccaskill-encourages-men-to-just-shut-the-hell-up_us_5642208ce4b0b24aee4be8ac.

Cornell Law Legal Information Institute. "Homicide." Accessed December 10, 2015. https://www.law.cornell.edu/wex/homicide.

Ertelt, Steven. "Woman Behind Roe V. Wade." LifeSiteNews, January 2013. Accessed December 10, 2015. http://www.lifenews.com/2013/01/22/woman-behind-roe-v-wade-im-dedicating-my-life-to-overturning-it/.

"Fetal Pain: The Evidence." Accessed December 10, 2015. http://www.doctorsonfetalpain.com/.

Last, Jonathan. "America's Baby Bust." Wall Street Journal (February 2013): 1. www.wsj.com/articles/

SB100014241278873233752045782700533877707
718

PBS. "People & Events: Eugenics and Birth Control." Accessed March 11, 2016. http://www.pbs.org/wgbh/amex/pill/peopleevents/e_eugenics.html.

Planned Parenthood. "Abortion." Accessed December 10, 2015. https://www.plannedparenthood.org/learn/abortion.

Zacharias, Ravi. "Twitter." Twitter. August 22, 2015. Accessed December 10, 2015. https://twitter.com/ravizacharias/status/635099200347201537.